This book belongs to:

HIP SURGERY?
NO PROBLLAMA

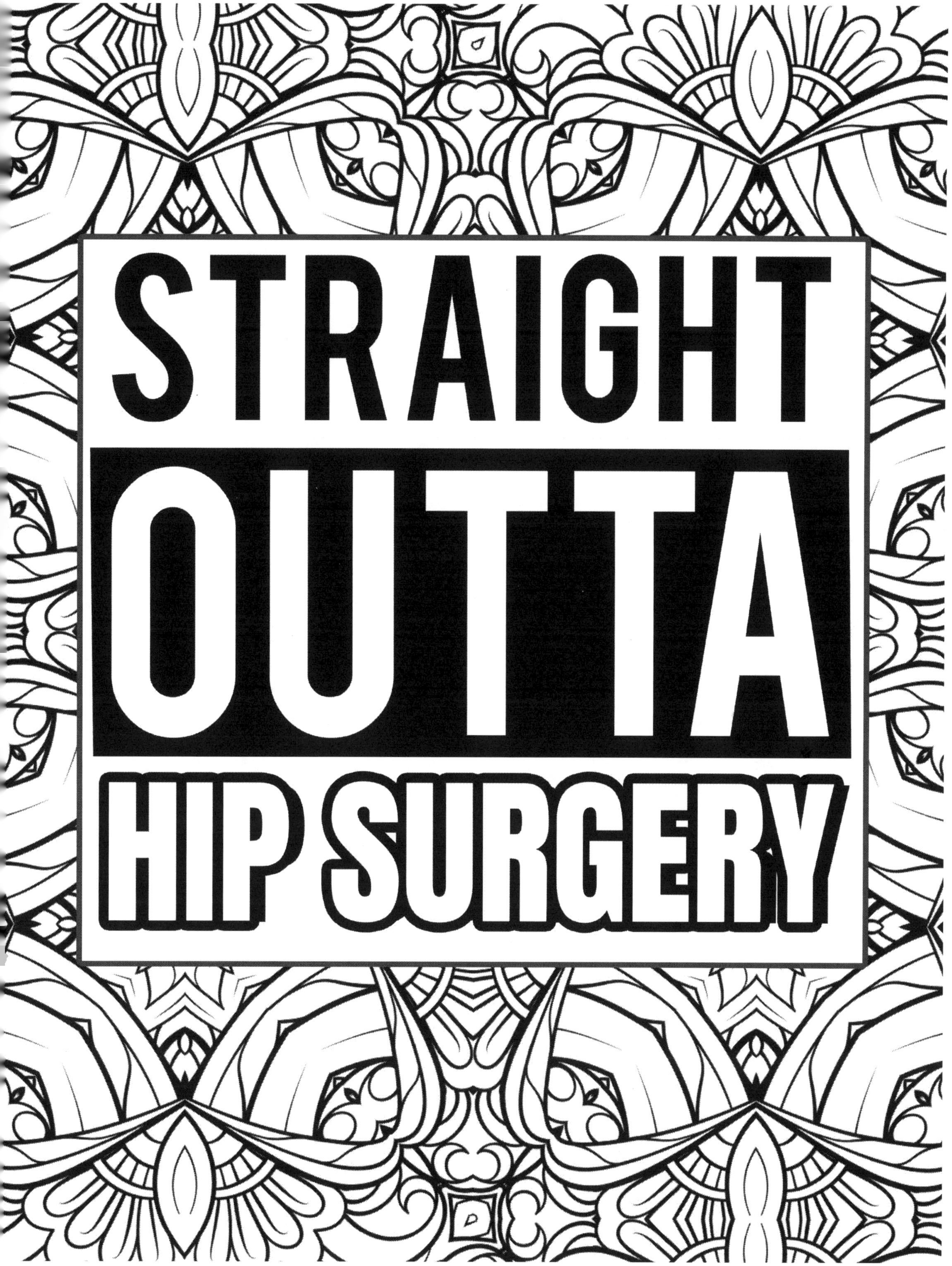
STRAIGHT
OUTTA
HIP SURGERY

YOU HAVE
NO IDEA
HOW STRONG
YOU ARE

HIP SURGERY
NOT FOR THE WEAK

Hip Hip
HOORAY
NO MORE TWINGES
IN THE
Hinges

DON'T MESS
WITH ME
I HAVE
BRAND NEW
HIP
AND I'M READY TO
RUMBLE

You
DON'T KNOW
how
STRONG
YOU ARE
UNTIL BEIN
Strong
is THE ONLY
CHOICE YOU HAVE

MAKE MY
HIP
GREAT AGAIN

Hip surgery
Recovery

BIONIC
WOMAN

I FLOCKING
Love
MY NEW
Hip

NEVER
UNDERESTIMATE
a woman
WITH A
NEW HIP

Hipster

SURGERY
RECOVERY
LOADING...

I JUST HAD A
JOINT
(REPLACEMENT)

Self Healing

NEW
HIP
NEW
ME

Girl,
YOU HAVE
NO IDEA
how
STRONG
YOU ARE

Get well soon

Made in the USA
Las Vegas, NV
20 March 2025

19849763R00024